Date Due	
NOV 1 1 2002	
NOV 1 4 2005	

Wood-Notes Wild

❧ WALKING
WITH
THOREAU

Selected by Mary Kullberg

Drawings by Christine Stetter

Southern Illinois
University Press
Carbondale and Edwardsville

Library of Congress Cataloging-in-Publication Data

Thoreau, Henry David, 1817–1862.
    [Selections. 1995]
    Wood-notes wild: walking with Thoreau / selected by Mary Kullberg;
    drawings by Christine Stetter.
      p. cm.
    I. Thoreau, Henry David, 1817–1862—Quotations. 2. Nature—
    Quotations, maxims, etc. 3. Quotations, American. I. Kullberg,
    Mary E. II. Stetter, Christine, date. III. Title.
    PS3042.K85 1995
    818,303—dc20
    ISBN 0-8093-1988-8   94-33389
                              CIP

6-5-00

19.95

For all those who share Thoreau's feelings for the earth, and especially for my grandchildren, Christopher, Carl, Wendy, Calvin, and Paul

Contents

I come to my solitary woodland walk
as the homesick go home. I thus
dispose of the superfluous
and see things as they are,
grand and beautiful.

—*Henry David Thoreau*

Preface

THOREAU IS WELL KNOWN AS THE WRITER who built a cabin by the side of Walden Pond in Concord, Massachusetts, living with nature for a little over two years, and whose eloquent and famous book, *Walden,* emanated from this experience. It is not so well known, however, that Thoreau lived in this Concord area most of his life and that for twenty-four years—from 1837 to 1861—took walks for "four hours a day at least," according to Thoreau, exploring the woods, fields, ponds, and rivers of the area. He carried a homemade notebook and took notes as he traveled, expanding them at home, usually in the morning, for his journal. Being a handwritten record of Thoreau's daily walks and thoughts, the journal had a spontaneous style, often with dashes between sentences and inconsistent capitalizations, as of the word *nature.* When separate but related passages were taken from the journal for his lectures, essays, or books, which was his usual procedure, Thoreau edited and polished them.

As Thoreau began to consider his journal less of a writer's workbook and more of an independent composition, it became his major literary goal. Having given up the school he headed with his brother, John, after John's death, Thoreau now surveyed land, lectured, tutored, and made pencils in his father's pencil factory, but only enough for subsistence so he could continue his walks and his writing. First published posthumously in 1906 in a fourteen-volume edition, *The Journal of Henry D. Thoreau* shows Thoreau's close relationship with nature; however, the journal's two million words—sometimes descriptive, sometimes literary, scientific, philosophical, or neighborhood-newsy—present a formidable undertaking for the reader. Taking excerpts from his journal and a few from his essays, books, and letters, I have created a typical year of Thoreau's nature experiences for *Wood-Notes Wild: Walking with Thoreau*. The title *Wood-Notes Wild* comes from a letter written to Thoreau by Horace Greeley, his literary agent, in which Greeley asked, "Would you like to swap some of your 'wood-notes wild' for dollars?" This book depicts through Thoreau's eyes not only the beauty of nature and the joy that can be found by being a part of it but Thoreau's feeling of coexistence with nature; Thoreau recognized the importance of each natural entity and its relatedness to the total habitat, the earth. Such a relationship is the underlying theme of the journal, the weft through which the journal fabric is woven.

William Channing, a poet and walking friend, wrote of Thoreau, "He did not walk with any view to health, or exercise, or amusement . . . the walk, with him, was for work; it had a serious purpose . . . his habit of mind demanded complete accuracy, the utmost finish, and that nothing should be taken on hearsay; believing that Nature . . . could not otherwise be reported . . . His calendar embraced cold and heat, rain and snow, ice and water . . . Night and the stars were not neglected friends." Bronson Alcott, another of his friends, gave this description of him: "Thoreau is himself a wood and its inhabitants. There is more in him of sod and shade and sky lights, of the genuine mold and moistures of the green gray earth, than in any person I know." Ralph Waldo Emerson, Thoreau's mentor and friend, whose first published book was entitled *Nature*, said, "Thoreau gives me, in flesh and blood . . . my own ethics. He is far more real, in daily practically obeying them, than I." And in his eulogy for Thoreau, Emerson said, "It was a pleasure and a privilege to walk with him. He knew the country like a fox or a bird, and passed through it as freely by paths of his own. He knew every track in the snow or on the ground, and what creature had taken the path before him . . . His power of observation seemed to indicate additional senses . . . One must submit abjectly to such a guide, and the reward was great." This is the Thoreau his closest friends knew, brother to the trees, the sun and stars, the rocks, the ponds and rivers, the birds and animals—an exuberant man who felt such a kinship with the earth that he could be no other place but with nature.

We are becoming a people separated from nature. To break the bond with nature is to stifle the spirit. We need nature to refresh us, to help us maintain our sense of composure and a proper perspective in a fast-paced, materialistic world. We are losers in even another way when we live apart from nature, for when we feel no relatedness to the earth, we feel no concern about such occurrences as species extinction or the loss of a rain forest, and our environment suffers. All this Thoreau seemed to know instinctively. Now considered one of the pioneers of the present environmental movement, Thoreau is credited for his vision and concern for the earth.

Wood-Notes Wild: Walking with Thoreau gives you the opportunity to be his walking friend and to share his thoughts as he joyously celebrates nature.

Mary Kullberg

Wood-Notes Wild

Spring

This is the first really spring day . . .
Something analogous to the thawing of the
ice seems to have taken place in the air.

The combination of this delicious air, which you do
not want to be warmer or softer, with the presence
of ice and snow, this is the charm of these days.

It is the summer beginning
to show itself in the midst
of winter.

Walking by the river . . . the black waves
yellowish where they break over ice—
I inhale a fresh, meadowy, spring odor . . .
which is a little exciting.

I sit on the bank at the Hemlocks and watch
the great white cakes of ice going swiftly by.
Now one strikes a rock and swings round in an eddy.

That dark-eyed water . . . is it
not the first sign of spring?

I thought I would follow down the
shallow gully through the woods . . .
that I might find more or something else.

> . . . sinking at each step deep into the thawing
> earth, gladly breaking through the gray rotting
> ice. The dullest sounds seem sweetly modulated
> by the air.

That dull-gray-barked willow shows its
silvery down of forthcoming catkins . . .

. . . the clear sap trickling from the red maple.

. . . brilliant spotted tortoises stirring
at the bottom of ditches.

I frequently see where oak leaves, absorbing
the heat of the sun, have sunk into the ice an
inch in depth and afterward have been blown out,
leaving a perfect type of the leaf.

When I get two-thirds up the hill I look round . . .
surprised by the landscape of the river valley and
the horizon with its distant blue scalloped rim—
It is a spring landscape . . . a deeper and warmer
blue than in winter . . .

I listen in vain to hear a frog
or a new bird . . . only the frozen
ground is melting a little deeper,
and water is trickling down the hills . . .

I find a place on the south side of this
rocky hill where the snow is melted and the
bare gray rock appears, covered with mosses
and lichens, where I can sit . . .

Some chickadees come flitting close to
me, and one utters its spring note . . .
for which I feel under obligation to him.

The earth I tread on is not a dead, inert mass.
It is a body, has a spirit, is organic, and fluid
to the influence of its spirit, and to whatever
particle of that spirit is in me.

As soon as I can get it painted
and dried, I launch my boat and make my
first voyage for the year up or down the
stream from which I have been debarred for
three months and a half.

Its surface is lit up here and there
with a fine-grained silvery sparkle
which makes the river appear something
celestial . . .

Looking through this transparent vapor,
all surfaces, not osiers and open water
alone, look more vivid. The hardness
of winter is relaxed.

The note of the first bluebird
answers to the purling rill of
melted snow . . . It is the accent
of the south wind.

Hundreds of tortoises, painted and wood,
are heard hurrying through the dry leaves
on the bank, and seen tumbling into the
water as my boat approaches . . .

When I examine a flat, sandy shore on which the
ripples now break, I find the tracks of many little
animals . . . the moist sand and mud which the water
has but ceased to dash over retains the most
delicate impressions.

The redwing and song sparrow are singing, and a flock of tree sparrows is pleasantly warbling.

> . . . suddenly, in some fortunate moment, the voice of eternal wisdom reaches me, even in the strain of a sparrow, and liberates me, whets and clarifies my senses, makes me a competent witness.

I hear one hyla peep faintly several times . . . He is the first of his race to awaken to the new year and pierce the solitude with his voice. He shall wear the medal for the year.

> You hear him, but you will never find him. He is somewhere down amid the withered sedge and alder bushes there by the water's edge, but where?

. . . I saw the blue heron arise from the shore . . .
with a great slate-colored expanse of wing,
suited to the shadows of the stream—a tempered
blue as of the sky and dark water commingled.

I see that it was made for these shallows,
and they for it. Now the heron has gone
from the weedy shoal, the scene appears
incomplete . . .

The heron uses these shallows as
I cannot. I give them up to him.

. . . like steel in different lights, the surface
of the still, living water . . . reflecting the
weeds and trees and now the warm colors of the
sunset sky!

Why should just these sights and
sounds accompany our life? . . . I
would fain explore the mysterious
relation between myself and these
things.

Now I have reached the hilltop . . .
and all around me is a sea of fog . . .
a glorious ocean after a storm, just lit by the
rising sun!

The sonorous, wavering sounds of these geese are
the voice of this cloudy air—an aerial sound and
yet so distinct . . . a clanking chain drawn through
the heavy air.

It is worth the while to walk today to hear
the rumbling roar of the wind . . . and when you pass
under the trees, oaks or elms that overhang the
road, the sound is more grand and stormy still . . .

I see the tawny and brown earth,
the fescue- and lichen-clad hills . . .

There is nothing more affecting and beautiful . . .
than the sight of the naked soil in the spring.

I am kin to the sod . . .

I see, on the southeast side of the blue-curls,
very distinct and regular arcs of circles . . .
scored deep in the sand by the tops of these
weeds which have been blown about by the wind.

No sooner has the ice of Walden melted than
the wind begins to play in dark ripples over
the surface . . .

There is life in these fresh
and varied colors, life in the
motion of the wind and the waves . . .

I hear a wood thrush, with a fine metallic
ring to his note. This sound most adequately
expresses the immortal beauty and wildness
of the woods. I go in search of him.

I will wander further from what I have called
my home—to the home which is forever inviting me.
In such an hour the freedom of the woods is
offered me, and the birds sing my dispensation.

I went through the swamp, and the yellow birches
sent forth a dull-yellow gleam which each time
made my heart beat faster . . .

I walked with the yellow birch.

Heard two hawks scream. There was something
truly March-like in it . . . a whistling of the
wind through a crevice in the sky, which, like
a cracked blue saucer, overlaps the woods.

The hawk is aerial brother
of the wave which he sails over
and surveys . . .

The gentle, springlike rain begins . . .
The sound of it pattering on dry oak leaves . . .
is just like that of wind stirring them.

You are more than paid for a wet coat and feet,
not only by the exhilaration that the fertile
moist air imparts, but by the increased fragrance
and more gem-like character of expanding buds and
leaflets in the rain.

And then the rain comes thicker and faster than before, thawing the remaining frost in the ground, detaining the migrating bird; and you turn your back to it, full of serene, contented thought, soothed by the steady dropping on the withered leaves.

You cannot go home yet;
you stay and sit in the rain.

About 9 PM I went to the edge of the river
to hear the frogs . . . They express, as it were,
the very feelings of the earth . . .

We must go out and re-ally ourselves to nature . . .
we must make root, send out some little fibre
at least.

A robin sings when I, in the house,
cannot distinguish the earliest dawning from the full
moonlight . . . I yielded the point to him, believing he
was better acquainted with the signs of the day than I.

I take all these walks to every point
of the compass. It is always harvest-time
with me. I am always gathering my
crop from these woods and fields
and waters.

My work is writing . . .
and no experience is too
trivial for me . . .

I am eager to report the glory of the
universe; may I be worthy to do it.

It is what I call a *washing* day . . . an agreeably
cool and clear and breezy day, when all things
appear as if washed bright and shiny . . .

The sound of the wind rustling the leaves is like
the rippling of a stream, and you see the light-
colored underside of the still fresh foliage, and
a sheeny light is reflected from the bent grass in
the meadow.

I scare up the great bittern in
a meadow by the Heywood Brook
near the ivy. He rises buoyantly
as he flies against the wind, and
sweeps south over the willow.

Saw a woodchuck, the first of the season . . . I ran up
within three feet of him . . . His eyes were a dull black
and rather inobvious, with a faint chestnut iris . . .
He would not stir as long as I was looking at him . . .

I respect him as one of the natives. He lies there,
by his color and habits so naturalized amid the dry
leaves, the withered grass, and the bushes . . . I think
I might learn some wisdom from him.

There suddenly flits before me . . .
a splendid purple finch. Its glowing
redness is revealed when it lifts its
wings, as when the ashes are blown
from a coal of fire.

There is always a kind of aeolian harp music
to be heard in the air. I hear it now, as it
were, the mellow sound of distant horns in the
hollow mansions of the upper air . . . and from
time to time this man or that hears it, having
ears that were made for music.

Saw a little skunk coming up the river-
bank in the woods . . . a funny little fellow,
about six inches long and nearly as broad.
It faced me and actually compelled me to
retreat before it for five minutes. Perhaps
I was between it and its hole.

The ring of toads, the note of the yellowbird, the
rich warble of the redwing, the thrasher on the hillside,
the robin's evening song, a woodpecker tapping some dead
tree across the water . . . I must make haste and go out on
the water.

I love to paddle now at
evening when the water is
smooth and the air begins
to be warm.

The air is full of the
fragrance of willow leaves . . .

The first bat goes suddenly zigzag
overhead . . . comes out of the dusk
and disappears into it.

A faint croaking from over the meadow . . .

It is candlelight. The fishes leap. The meadows sparkle with the coppery light of fireflies.

The evening star, multiplied by undulating water, is like bright sparks of fire continually ascending.

The reflections of the trees are grandly
indistinct. There is a low mist slightly
enlarging the river, through which the
arches of the stone bridge are just visible . . .

There is a low crescent of northern lights
and shooting stars from time to time . . .

. . . the scent of muskrats . . .
In the faint reflected twilight I distinguish
one rapidly swimming away from me, leaving a
widening ripple behind, and now hear one plunge
from some willow or rock.

I take infinite pains to know all the phenomena
of the spring, for instance, thinking that I have
here the entire poem, but then, to my chagrin, I
hear that it is but an imperfect copy that I
possess and have read, but my ancestors have torn
out many of the first leaves and grandest passages . . .
I wish to know an entire heaven and an entire earth.

Summer

Already the aspens are trembling
again, and a new summer is offered me.

The pond is perfectly smooth and very beautiful now.
Its shores are still almost entirely uninjured by
the axe . . . We took an old leaky boat and a forked stick,
which had made part of a fence, and pushed out to see
the shores from the middle of the pond.

The forest has never so good a setting,
nor is so distinctly beautiful as when
seen from the middle of a small lake amid
hills which rise from the water's edge.

The blue flag grows in this pure
water, rising from the stony bottom
all around the shore, and is very
beautiful . . . especially its reflections
in the water . . .

    I am that rock by
    the pondside.

Our boat leaked so—faster and
faster as it sank deeper and tipped
with the water in it—that we were
obliged to return to the shore.

With our boat's prow to the shore,
we sat half an hour, listening to
the bullfrogs.

The bullfrogs begin with one or two notes and with each
peal add another trill to their trump—er-roonk, er-er-roonk,
er-er-er-roonk. I am amused to hear one after another, and
then an unexpectedly deep and confident bass . . . And now, as
if by a general agreement, they all trump together, making a
deafening noise. Sometimes one jumps up a foot out of the
water in the midst of these concerts.

. . . those little striped breams
poised in Walden's glaucous water . . .

I have thus stood over them half an
hour at a time and stroked them
familiarly without frightening them,
suffering them to nibble my fingers
harmlessly . . . and have even taken them
out of the water with my hand . . .

. . . the miracle of its existence: my
contemporary and neighbor, yet so different
from me! I can only poise my thought
there by its side and try to think like a bream
for a moment . . . Acquaintance with it is to
make my life more rich and eventful.

Blue-eyed grass now begins to give
that slaty-blue tint to the meadow.

    I to be Nature . . . as the blue-eyed grass
    in the meadow looks into the face of
    the sky.

Going through Britton's clearing, I find a black
snake out enjoying the sun. I perceive his
lustrous greenish blackness. He holds up his head
and threatens; then dashes off into the woods, making
a great rustling among the leaves.

Saw my white-headed eagle again . . . He was first
flying low over the water; then rose gradually
and circled westward toward White Pond . . . He
rose high at last, till I almost lost him in
the clouds.

The earth is not a mere fragment
of dead history . . . but living poetry . . .

I hear my hooting owl
now just before sunset.

The sun is gone. An amber light and golden
glow . . . The redness now begins to fade on
eastern clouds, and the western cloudlets glow
with burnished copper alloyed with gold . . .

It is perfectly warm and I am tempted to
stay out all night and observe each phenomenon
of the night until day dawns . . .

Now the first whippoorwill sings hollowly in the
woods . . . and now, when we thought the daybirds gone
to roost, the wood thrush takes up the strain.

> The bullfrogs trump . . .
> Night is seen settling down
> with mists on the bay.

The pitch pine woods are heavy and dark,
but the river is full of golden light . . .
You see the first star in the southwest,
and know not how much earlier you might
have seen it had you looked.

. . . the night-hawk dashes past in the twilight
with mottled wing, within a rod of me.

As the twilight deepens and the moonlight is
more and more bright, I begin to distinguish
myself, who I am and where; as my walls contract
I become more collected and composed and sensible
of my own existence, as when a lamp is
brought into a dark apartment.

The very wind on my cheek
seems more fraught with meaning.

I sit awhile in the shade of the woods
and look out on the moonlit fields.

. . . streaks of light on the edge of the path . . .
all these leaves so still . . . no birds in motion—
how can I be else than still and thoughtful?

How dark the shadows of the pine
and oaks fall across the woodland path!
It is pleasant walking in these forest
paths, with heavy darkness on one side
and a silvery moonlight on the other.
How picturesque the moonlight on rocks
in the woods!

I go and come with a strange sense of liberty
in Nature, a part of herself.

I do not see that I can live tolerably without
affection for Nature. If I feel no softening
toward the rocks, what do they signify?

Looking down from the Cliffs the leaves of the
treetops shine more than ever by day—here and
there a lightning bug shows his greenish light
over the tops of the trees . . .

Returning down the hill by the path to where
the woods cut off . . .

> . . . there is a yellowish segment
> of light in the east, paling a star
> and adding sensibly to the light of
> the waning and now declining moon.

Sunrise. I see it gliding the top of the hill
behind me . . . there is something serenely glorious
and memorable to me in the sight of the first
cool sunlight.

In order to avoid delusions I would fain let man
go by, and behold a universe in which man is but as
a grain of sand.

It is a good day to saunter.

Where my path crosses the brook
in the meadow there is a singularly
sweet scent in the heavy air . . .
the fragrance of the earth . . .

A small brown grasshopper jumps
into the brook at our approach and,
drifting down, clings to a stubble.

I love to follow up the course of the
brook and see the cardinal flowers which
stand in its midst above the rocks.

I observed a middling-sized red oak . . . with
a pretty large hole in one side about fifteen
feet from the ground . . . So I shinnied up, and
when I reached up one hand to the hole to pull
myself up by it, the thought passed through my
mind that perhaps something may take hold of my fingers,
but nothing did . . .

I looked in, and to my great surprise, there squatted
a salmon-brown bird . . . seemingly asleep . . . and close
to my face. It was a minute or two before I made it
out to be an owl . . . After a little while I put in one
hand and stroked it repeatedly, whereupon it reclined
its head a little lower and closed its eyes entirely.

. . . the lupine is now in its glory. It paints
a whole hillside with its blue.

. . . the bushes are black with huckleberries. They
droop over the rocks with the weight . . . some glossy
black, some dull black, some blue.

I am interested in each contemporary plant in my
vicinity . . . They are cohabitants with me of this
part of the planet . . .

I see the fringed purple orchis, unexpectedly
beautiful . . . a large spike of purple flowers . . .

In an open part of the swamp, started a very
large wood frog, which gave one leap and squatted
still. I put down my finger, and though it
shrank a little at first, it permitted me to
stroke it as I pleased.

Having passed, it occurred to me to return and
cultivate its acquaintance. To my surprise, it
allowed me to slide my hand under it and lift it up . . .

It was . . . not the dull dead-leaf color which I had
imagined, but its back was like burnished bronze
armor . . . It had four or five dusky bars which matched
exactly when the legs were folded, showing that the
painter applied his brush to the animal when in that
position, and reddish-orange soles to its delicate
feet.

Here is home; the beauty of the world impresses you. There is a coolness in your mind as in a well. Life is too grand for supper.

While I write here, I hear the foxes trotting about me over the dead leaves, and now gently over the grass, as if not to disturb dew which is falling.

> I give up to him sun and earth
> as to their true proprietor.

And now the first star is lit, and I go home.

The river appears covered
with an almost imperceptible blue film.
The sun is not yet over the bank . . .
There is music in every sound in the
morning atmosphere.

> I have passed down the river before
> sunrise on a summer morning between
> fields of water lilies still shut in
> sleep; and when . . . sunlight from over the
> bank fell on the surface of the water,
> whole fields of white blossoms seemed to
> flash open before me as I floated along,
> like the unfolding of a banner.

Look toward the sun, the water is yellow . . .
look from the sun and it is a beautiful dark blue;
but in each direction the crests of the waves are
white and you cannot sail or row over this watery
wilderness without sharing the excitement.

There go a couple of ducks, which probably
I have started . . . with a slight descent in
their low flight toward a new cove.

That duck was all jewels combined, showing
different lustres as it turned on the unrippled
element in various lights, now
brilliant mossy green, now dusky violet, now
a rich bronze, now the reflections that sleep
in the ruby's grain.

We need the tonic of wildness, to wade
sometimes in marshes where the bittern and
the meadow hen lurk, and hear the blooming
of the snipe; to smell the whispering sedge
where only some wilder and more solitary
fowl builds her nest, and the mink crawls
with its belly close to the ground.

Now I see a great dark low-arching cloud
in the northwest already dropping rain
there and steadily sweeping southeast . . . the
rest of the sky is quite serene.

. . . the rush of the cool wind while the
thunder is yet scarcely audible. The flashes . . .
lighting up different parts of the horizon—
now the edges of the cloud, now far along the
horizon—showing a clearer golden space beneath
the cloud where the rain is falling . . .

Suddenly comes the gust, and the big drops slanting
from the north, and the birds fly as if rudderless,
and the trees bow and are wrenched.

. . . we in haste drew up our boat . . . upset it and got
under, sitting on the paddles. It was very pleasant
to lie there half an hour close to the edge of the
water and see and hear the great drops patter on the
river, each making a great bubble.

The far retreated thunder clouds in
the southeast horizon . . . emitting low
flashes which reveal their forms . . .

The life, the joy that is in
blue sky after a storm!

I pick raspberries dripping with
rain beyond Sleepy Hollow.

I wish so to live . . . as to derive my satisfaction and
inspirations from the commonest events, everyday
phenomenon.

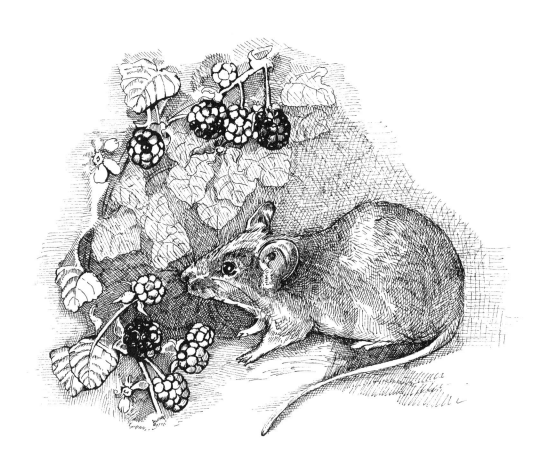

Autumn

How long is it since I heard a veery?
Do they go, or become silent, when the gold-finch
heralds the autumn?

I felt my spirits rise when I had got off the road
into the open fields. And the sky had a new
appearance. I stepped along more buoyantly.

Examined my old friend the green
locust shrilling on an alder leaf.

I find the mud turtle's eggs all hatched . . .
there is, however, one still left in the nest . . .
I took out this remaining one, which perhaps,
could not get out alone, and it began slowly to
crawl toward the brook . . . Now and then it paused,
stretched out its head, looked around and appeared
to be deliberating . . .
It was so slow that I could not stop to watch it,
and so carried it to within seven or eight inches
of the water . . .

Now is the time for chestnuts. A stone cast against
the tree shakes them down in showers upon one's head
and shoulders. But I cannot excuse myself for using
the stone . . . I sympathize with the tree, yet I
heaved a big stone against the trunk . . . I was as
affected as if I had cast a rock at a sentient being.

We shall purely use the earth
and not abuse it . . .

. . . the seeds of the milkweed . . .

I released some seeds with the long, fine silk
attached. The fine threads fly apart at once,
open with a spring, and then ray themselves out
into a hemispherical form, each thread freeing
itself from its neighbor and all reflecting
prismatic or rainbow tints.

To be serene and successful we must
be at one with the universe.

The winds of autumn begin to blow.
Now I can sail.

> I rigged my mast by putting a post across
> the boat, and putting the mast through it and
> into a piece of a post at the bottom, and
> lashing and bracing it . . .

I find my boat all covered, bottom and seats, with
the leaves of the golden willow . . . I set sail with a
cargo of them rustling under my feet.

What an entertainment this river affords! It is subject to great overflows, owing to its broad intervals, that a day's rain produces a new landscape . . . I sail with a smacking breeze today, and fancy that I am a sailor on the ocean.

The sun is in my face and the waves look particularly lively and sparkling . . . The waves seem to leap and roll like porpoises, with a slight surging sound when their crests break . . . It is pleasant, exhilarating, to feel the boat tossed . . .

Brought home quite a boat-load of fuel—one oak
rail . . . a white pine rider with a square hole in
it made by a woodpecker . . . several chestnut rails . . .
a large oak stump which I know to have been bleaching
for more than thirty years, with great gray
prongs sprinkled with lichens.

> . . . I derive a separate and peculiar
> pleasure from every stick that I find.
> Each has its history, of which I am
> reminded when I come to burn it, and
> under what circumstances I found it.

. . . the steady, soaking, rushing sound of the rain on the shingles is musical . . . It is because I am allied to the elements that the sound of the rain is thus soothing to me. The sound soaks into my spirit, as the water into the earth.

How plainly we are
a part of nature.

It is a beautiful Indian summer
day . . . it is akin to sin to spend such a
day in the house.

Birches, hickories, aspens . . . are like
innumerable small flames on the hillsides
about the pond. The pond is now most
beautifully framed with the autumn-tinted
woods and hills.

> . . . the reflections are never purer
> or more distinct than now at the
> season of the fall of the leaf . . .

I pick up a white oak leaf, dry and
stiff, but yet mingled red and green,
October-like, whose pulpy part some
insect has eaten . . . exposing the delicate
network of its veins. It is very
beautiful held up to the light.

Shall I not have intelligence with
the earth? Am I not partly leaves
and vegetable mould myself?

The pickerel of Walden!
. . . They are not green like the
pines or gray like the stones, or
blue like the sky but they have . . .
to my eye, yet rarer colors like
precious stones.

It is the poetry of fishes
which is their chief use . . .

I returned by the west side of Lee's Cliff hill,
and sit on a rounded rock . . . covered with fresh-
fallen pine needles . . .

The mountains are white with snow . . .
The edges of the mountains now melt
into the sky.

I see numerous butterflies still,
yellow and small red . . .

. . . examined a hornet's nest . . . no
hornets buzzing around it.

The wild apples are now getting palatable.
I find a few left on distant trees which the
farmer thinks it not worth his while to gather.
He thinks that he has better in his barrels,
but he is mistaken, unless he has a walker's
appetite and imagination . . .

The age of miracles is each moment thus
returned. Now it is wild apples, now
river reflections, now a flock of lesser
redpolls.

It is but mid-afternoon when I see the
sun setting far through the woods . . . that
peculiar clear vitreous greenish sky in the
west, as it were a molten gem.

When I play my flute tonight . . . I hear an echo
from a neighboring wood, a stolen pleasure.

The fragrance of the apple in my pocket has,
I confess, deterred me from eating it.

It is a full moon and a clear night with a strong
northwest wind . . . We sail rapidly upward . . . Venus
remarkably bright . . . Not a cloud in the sky, only
the moon and a few faint unobtrusive stars here and
there, and from time to time a meteor.

It is very pleasant to make our way thus rapidly but
mysteriously over the black waves . . . not knowing
where you are exactly, only avoiding shores.

The glory of November is in its silvery,
sparkling lights . . . to walk over bare pastures and
see the abundant sheeny light, like a universal
halo, reflected from the russet and bleached earth.

> . . . the trees so tidy and stripped
> of their leaves; the meadows and
> pastures clothed with clean dry
> grass, looking as if they had been
> swept; ice on the water and winter
> in the air . . .

Of thee, O earth, are my bone and sinew made;
to thee, O sun, am I brother . . .

The autumnal tints grow gradually
darker and duller, but not less rich
to my eye.

> The small red and yellow buds, the maze
> of gray twigs, the green and red sphagnum,
> the conspicuous yellowish buds of the swamp
> pink . . . the dried choke-berries . . . the cranberry
> rising red above the ice . . .

Picked up a pitch pine cone which had
evidently been cut off by a squirrel.

If you would be convinced how differently armed
the squirrel is naturally for dealing with
pitch pine cones, just try to get one off with
your teeth. He who extracts the seeds from a
single closed cone with the aid of a knife will
be constrained to confess that the squirrel
earns his dinner.

> The squirrel has the key
> to this conical and spiny chest . . .
> He sits on a post, vibrating his
> tail . . .

I feel slightly complimented when Nature condescends to make use of me without my knowledge, as when I help scatter her seeds in my walk, or carry burs and cockles on my clothes from field to field.

. . . a little brook of very cold spring water . . . with a gray sandy and pebbly bottom, flowing through this dense swampy thicket . . . The sun falls in here and there between the leaves and shines on its bottom . . . The trilliums on its brink have fallen into it and bathe their red berries in the water, waving in the stream . . . Here is a recess apparently never frequented.

> We need to witness . . .
> some life pasturing freely
> where we never wander.

Our woods are now so reduced that the chopping of this winter has been a cutting to the quick . . . They have even infringed fatally upon White Pond.

It is too cold today to use a paddle; the water freezes on the handle and numbs my fingers.

I love to have the river closed up for a season and a pause put to my boating. I shall launch it again in the spring with so much more pleasure. I love best to have each thing in its season only . . .

Winter

Every leaf and twig was this morning
covered with a sparkling ice armor; even the
grasses in exposed fields were hung with
innumerable diamond pendants . . .

What a crash of jewels as I walk!
The most careless walker who never
deigned to look at these humble weeds
before, cannot help observing them now.

In this clear and bright sunlight, the
ice-covered trees have new beauty, especially
the birches . . . bent quite to the ground.

Each ice-incrusted stubble shines like
a prism with some color of the rainbow—
intense blue, or violet, or red.

The whole hill is like an immense quartz rock,
with minute crystals sparkling from innumerable
crannies.

Such is beauty . . . If I seek her elsewhere
because I do not find her at home, my
search will prove a fruitless one.

. . . the unrelenting steel-cold scream of
a jay, unmelted, that never flows into a
song, a sort of winter trumpet, screaming
cold; hard tense frozen music, like the
winter sky itself . . .

. . . my eye rested with pleasure on
the white pines, now reflecting a
silvery light . . .

> Our lives need the relief of such a background,
> where the pine flourishes and a jay still screams.

I listen to the booming of the pond as if it were a
reasonable creature.

> I return at last in a rain,
> and am coated with a glaze,
> like the fields.

Tonight while I am arranging these sprigs
of white pine in my scrapbook I am reminded
by their fragrance of the pines and hemlocks
which overhang the river . . .

My wealth should be all in pine tree shillings.

Winter comes to make walking possible where there was no walking in summer. I may walk down the main river or up either of its two branches.

> The river is now completely concealed
> by snow. I come this way partly because
> it is the best walking here, the snow
> not so deep.

> I see that the fox has already taken the
> same walk before me, just along the edge of
> the button bushes . . . we both turn our steps
> hither at the same time.

> Why should we not cultivate neighborly
> relations with the foxes?

Two nuthatches . . . talking to each
other. One hung with his head down
on a large pitch pine, pecking
the bark for a long time.

    . . . the shrub oak rising above
the snow . . .

Tenacious of its leaves, which
shrivel not but retain a certain
winter life in them . . . well tanned
leather on the one side, sun-
tanned, color of colors—color of
the cow and the deer, silver-
downy beneath.

A rabbit scuds away over the crust.

On the ice at Walden are very
beautiful great leaf crystals . . .
they look like a loose web of
small white feathers springing
from a tuft of down.

It is a dark, transparent ice, but will not bear
me without much cracking . . . When I lie down on it
and examine it closely, I find that the greater part
of the bubbles . . . are against its under surface, and
that they are continually rising from the bottom—
perfect spheres . . . beautiful and clear, in which I
see my face . . .

It begins to snow hard . . . completely obscuring
the view through the aisles of the wood, and
in open fields it is rapidly drifting.

Examined closely, the flakes
are beautifully regular six-
rayed stars, or wheels with a
center disk, perfect geometric
figures.

Talk of mysteries! Think of
our life in nature—daily to be
shown matter, to come in contact
with it—rocks, trees, wind on
our cheeks! The solid earth!
the actual world!

The snow blows like spray, fifteen feet high, across
the fields while the wind roars in the trees as in
the rigging of a vessel . . . a solid column of snow six
or eight feet deep—the wind, eddying through and over
the wall, is scooping it out in fantastic forms . . .

With this snow the fences
are scarcely an obstruction . . .

I love to wade and flounder through the swamp
now, these bitter cold days when the snow lies
deep on the ground . . . I penetrate to islets
inaccessible in summer, my feet slumping to
the sphagnum far out of sight beneath . . .

> My seat from time to time
> is the springy horizontal bough
> of some fallen tree which is frozen
> into the ice, some old maple that
> has blown over . . .

And now the snow has ceased . . .

As you walk in the woods you hear
the rustling sound of limbs and
leaves that are relieved of their
burden—and of the falling snow.

> . . . there is scarcely a track of any
> animal yet to be seen, except here
> and there the surface of the snow has
> been raised where some mouse came
> near the surface in its travels . . .

Joy and sorrow, success and failure, grandeur and
meanness, and indeed most words in the English
language, do not mean for me what they do for my
neighbors.

To make a perfect day like this, you must
have a clear, sparkling air, with a sheen from the
snow, sufficient cold, little or no wind; and the
warmth must come directly from the sun. It must not
be a thawing warmth.

The clouds reflecting a dazzling
brightness from their edges . . .
some most brilliant mother-of-pearl.

I get away a mile or two from the town into
the stillness and solitude of nature, with rocks,
trees, weeds, snow about me . . . it is as I had come
to an open window. I see out and around myself . . .

How glorious the perfect stillness
and peace of the winter landscape.

Just this side of Bittern Cliff I see
a very remarkable track of an otter . . .

I saw where they had been playing,
sliding, or fishing, apparently today,
on the snow-covered rocks . . .

. . . when I consider that the nobler animals have
been exterminated here—the cougar, panther,
lynx, wolverine, wolf, bear, moose, deer, the
beaver, the turkey, etc.,—I cannot but feel as
if I live in a tamed and, as it were, emasculated
country. Would not the motions of those larger
and wilder animals have been more significant
still?

A little further I heard the sound
of a downy woodpecker tapping a pitch
pine in a little grove, and saw him
inclining to dodge behind the stem. He
flitted from pine to pine before me.

> . . . then the whir of a partridge on or
> beneath an old decaying apple tree which the
> pines surrounded . . . I saw one's track under
> an apple tree and where it had pecked a
> frozen-thawed apple.

Returning just before sunset, I see the ice
beginning to be green, and a rose color reflected
from the low snow patches . . . When crossing
Hubbard's broad meadow, the snow patches are a
most beautiful crystalline purple, like the petals
of some flowers . . . It would not be more
enchanting to walk amid the purple clouds of
the sunset sky.

My home is as much of nature as my heart embraces
If I only warm my house, then is that only my
home. But if I sympathize with the heats and
colds, the sounds and silence of nature and share
the repose and equanimity that reign around me in
the fields, then they are my house . . .

Snowed again half an inch in the evening, after which,
at ten o'clock, the moon still obscured, I skated on
the river . . . Our skates make but little sound in this
coating of snow . . . we can easily see our tracks in the
night. We seem thus to go faster than before by day . . .
because of the impression which the mysterious muffled
sound our feet make . . .

Yesterday I skated after a fox over the ice. Occasionally
he sat on his haunches and barked at me like a young wolf . . .
The fox manifested an almost human suspicion of mystery in
my actions.

> When I skated directly after him, he cantered
> at the top of his speed; but when I stood still,
> though his fear was not abated, some strange but
> inflexible law of his nature caused him to stop
> also, and sit again on his haunches.

I have been surveying for 20 or 30 days . . .
and tonight for the first time have made a fire in
my chamber and endeavored to return to myself. I
wish to do again . . . things quite congenial to my
highest inmost and most sacred nature—to lurk in
crystalline thought like the trout under verdurous
banks . . .

It seems an age since I took walks and wrote in my
journal . . .

I long for wildness, a nature which I cannot put
my foot through, woods where the wood thrush forever
sings, where the hours are early morning ones
and there is dew on the grass . . . where I might have
a fertile unknown for a soil around me.

My pulse must beat with nature.

Fogs and rains and warmer suns are gradually melting the snow; the days have grown sensibly longer . . .

In this lonely glen with its brook draining the slopes, its creased ice and crystals of all hues, where the spruces and hemlocks stand up on either side and the rush and sere wild oats in the rivulet itself, our lives are more serene and worthy to contemplate.

We rejoice in the full rills, the melting
snow, the copious spring rains and the
freshets, as if we were frozen earth to be
thawed.

I see a large flock of sheldrakes, which
have probably risen from the pond, go over
my head in the woods . . . you hear the whistling
of their wings, and in a moment they are lost
in the horizon.

> . . . the river is no sooner fairly open
> than they are back again—before I
> have got my boat launched . . .

I hear faintly the cawing of a crow, far, far away,
echoing from some unseen woodside, as if deadened by
the spring-like vapor which the sun is drawing from
the ground . . . It is not merely crow calling to crow
for it speaks to me too. I am part of one great
creature with him.

This afternoon I throw off my outside coat . . .
I lean over a rail to hear what is in the air,
liquid with the bluebird's warble . . .

Perhaps there will be a time
when the bluebirds themselves
will not return any more.

I pray for such inward experience
as will make nature significant.

I wish to speak a word for Nature, for
absolute freedom and wildness . . . to regard man
as an inhabitant or part and parcel of Nature
rather than a member of society . . . there are
enough champions of civilization.

I will take another walk to the Cliff, another
row on the river, another skate on the meadow,
be out in the first snow, and associate with
the winter birds. Here I am at home. In the
bare and bleached crust of the earth, I recognize
my friend.

Sources

With the exception of those listed below, quotations are from *The Journal of Henry D. Thoreau, Vols. I–XIV*, Riverside Press, Houghton Mifflin, 1906. All page numbers refer to *Wood-Notes Wild*.

The Correspondence of Henry David Thoreau, edited by Walter Harding and Carl Bode, New York University Press, 1958:
I am kin to the sod . . .   p. 18

Familiar Letters of Henry David Thoreau, edited by F. B. Sanborn, Houghton Mifflin, 1894:
I to be Nature . . .   p. 41

The Maine Woods, Henry David Thoreau, edited by Joseph J. Moldenhauer, Princeton University Press, 1972:
Talk of mysteries . . .   p. 100

Pittsburgh Series in Bibliography: Henry David Thoreau, edited by Raymond R. Borst, University of Pittsburgh Press, 1981:
We shall purely use . . .   p. 68

Thoreau the Poet-Naturalist, William Channing, Charles E. Goodspeed, 1902 (from a letter to Daniel Ricketson):
Perhaps there will be . . .   p. 116

Walden, or Life in the Woods, Henry David Thoreau, Houghton Mifflin, 1893:

    The hawk is aerial brother . . .   p. 21

    I go and come . . .   p. 49

    We need the tonic of . . .   p. 62

    Shall I not have . . .   p. 75

    We need to witness . . .   p. 86

    Every leaf . . .   p. 89

A Week on the Concord and Merrimac Rivers, Henry David Thoreau, Holt, Rinehart and Winston, 1963:

    I have thus stood . . .   p. 40

    I have passed . . .   p. 59

    Our lives need . . .   p. 92

From the following Thoreau essays:

    "Autumnal Tints," *Atlantic Monthly,* 1862:

    I find my boat . . .   p. 70

"Natural History of Massachusetts," *The Dial,* 1842:

    I give up to him . . .   p. 58

"Walking," in *Essays, English and American,* Harvard Classics, vol. 28, Collier, 1910:

    I wish to speak . . .   p. 116

"A Winter Walk," *The Dial,* 1843:

    How glorious . . .   p. 106

    In this lonely glen . . .   p. 113

Preface quotations are from the following:

    "Walking" by Henry David Thoreau, in *Essays, English and American* (Harvard Classics, vol. 28, Collier, 1910); *The Correspondence of Henry*

David Thoreau, edited by Walter Harding and Carl Bode (New York University Press, 1958); *Thoreau the Poet-Naturalist* by William Channing (Charles E. Goodspeed, 1902); *The Journals of Bronson Alcott*, selected and edited by Odell Shepard (Little, Brown and Co., 1938); Paul Brooks's introduction to *Thoreau's Country* by H. W. Gleason, edited by Mark Silber (Sierra Club Books, 1975); and *Annotated Walden*, edited by Philip Van Doren Stern (C. N. Potter, 1970).

MARY KULLBERG is an author whose works include another compilation of Thoreau, *Morning Mist: Thoreau and Basho Through the Seasons,* and two children's books. A member of the Sierra Club, The Nature Conservancy, and the Audubon Society, Kullberg has a deep and enduring love of nature that has led to her interest in Thoreau. She and her ecologist husband reside in Cape Girardeau, Missouri, often traveling to natural areas of the country.

CHRISTINE I. STETTER is a natural science illustrator with five previous books to her credit. She presently serves as an artist with Texas A&M University.

COLOPHON

This book is set in Centaur type, a face designed by Bruce Rogers in 1929 and first cut by the English Monotype Corporation that year. The type, based on the 1470 types of Nicholas Jenson, is considered to be perhaps the finest work of American typographers, and is used here in its electronic version, which remains faithful to the original. This edition is printed on Mohawk Superfine vellum. The design of the book and jacket is the work of Gary Gore.